DEPARTURES

For Richard,
affectionstly,
Don Justin

Books by Donald Justice

Departures · 1973
Night Light · 1967
The Summer Anniversaries · 1959

Editor
Contemporary French Poetry
(with Alexander Aspel) · 1965
The Collected Poems of Weldon Kees · 1966

DONALD JUSTICE

DEPARTURES

Atheneum New York
1973

These poems first appeared in the following magazines:
American Poetry Review: *1971; After the Chinese.*
Antaeus: *Riddle.*
Ariel: *Fragment: To a Mirror.*
Contempora: *Portrait with Flashlight; Portrait with
    Tequila; Self-Portrait As Still Life; Pale Tepid Ode.*
The Iowa Review: *ABC; Portrait with One Eye; On the
    Night of the Departure by Bus; The Success; Poem.*
The New Yorker: *The Confession; An Elegy Is
    Preparing Itself.*
The North American Review: *Luxury; From a Note-
    book; Warm Flesh-Colored Ode.*
Kayak: *Things; Sonatina in Green.*
New American Review: *Cool Dark Ode; Variation on
    a Text by Vallejo.*
Poetry: *A Letter ; Portrait with Short Hair; Lethargy;
    White Notes; The Assassination.*
Seneca Review: *A Dancer's Life; The Telephone Num-
    ber of the Muse; Twenty Questions; Lorcaesques.*
Virginia Quarterly Review: *Homage to the Memory of
    Wallace Stevens.*

Originally published in a limited edition by The Stone
    Wall Press & The Penumbra Press, Iowa City, Iowa.

Library of Congress catalog card number 73-80748
ISBN 0-689-10568-1
Published simultaneously in Canada by
    McClelland and Stewart Ltd
Composition by Bonnie Pratt O'Connell and design
    of text by K.K. Merker
Manufactured by the Murray Printing Company,
    Forge Village, Massachusetts
First Atheneum Edition

. . . and somewhere among the remote and vaulted ceilings of just such stations the farewells of the dead must long ago have left behind their still slowly diminishing echo.

Contents

ONE

A

A syllable with skin,
  tough and saurian,
  alive in the sewer's mouth.

A word with loot
  bulging its pockets,
  crouched in the alley after curfew.

A whole stanza forming
  to march off the curb
  and into your head with banners.

A poem in hiding
  from men in advertising
  and the guitars of ex-pilots.

B

Be the unfolding page,
  white page, memorial to the absolute,
  atlas of heights and depths,

Be the statue leaning out from the stone,
  the stone also, torn between past and future,
  and the hammer, whose strength we share.

C

See how the fearful chandelier
  trembles above you
  each time you open your mouth
  to sing. Sing.

Fragment: To a Mirror

Behind that bland facade of yours,
What drafts are moving down what intricate maze
Of halls? What solitude of attics waits,
Bleak, at the top of the still hidden stair?
And are these windows yours that open out
On such spectacular views?
Those still bays yours, where small boats lie
At anchor, abandoned by their crews?
The parks nearby,
Whose statues doze forever in the sun?
Those stricken avenues,
Along which great palms wither and droop down
Their royal fronds,
And the parade is drummed
To a sudden, inexplicable halt?
                              Tell me,
Is this the promised absence I foresee
In you, when no breath any more shall stir
The milky surface of the sleeping pond,
And you shall have back your rest at last,
Your half of nothingness?

1963-1972

A Letter

You write that you are ill, confused. The trees
Outside the window of the room they gave you
Are wet with tears each morning when they wake you
Out of the sleep you never quite fall into,
For there's some dream of traffic in your head

That stops and goes, and goes, and does not stop
Sometimes all night, all day. The motorcade
Winds past you like the funeral cortege
Of someone famous you had slept with, once or twice.
(Another fit of tears dampens the leaves, the page.)

You would expose your wounds, pull down your blouse,
Unbosom yourself wholly to the young doctor
Who has the power to sign prescriptions, passes,
Who seems to like you . . . And so to pass
Into the city once again, one of us,

Hurrying by the damp trees of a park
Towards the familiar intersection where
A traffic signal warns you not to cross,
To wait, just as before, alone – but suddenly
Ten years older, tamed now, less mad, less beautiful.

A Dancer's Life

Homage to Bergman

The lights in the theater fail. The long racks
Of costumes abandoned by the other dancers
Trouble Celeste. The conductor asks
If she is sad because autumn is coming on,

But when autumn comes she is merely pregnant and bored.
On her way back from the holidays, a man
Who appears to have no face rattles the door
To her compartment. *How disgusting,* she thinks;

How disgusting it always must be to grow old.
Dusk falls, and a few drops of rain.
On the train window trembles the blurred
Reflection of her own transparent beauty,

And, through this, beautiful ruined cities passing,
Dark forests, and people everywhere
Pacing on lighted platforms, some
Beating their children, some apparently dancing.

The costumes of the dancers sway in the chill darkness.
Now sinking into sleep is like sinking again
Into the lake of her youth. Her parents
Lean from the rail of a ferryboat waving, waving,

As the boat glides farther out across the waves.
No one, it seems, is meeting her at the station.
The city is frozen. She warms herself
In the pink and scented twilight of a bar.

The waiter who serves her is young. She nods assent.
The conversation dies in bed. Later,
She hurries off to rehearsal. In the lobby,
Dizzy still with the weight of her own body,

She waits, surrounded by huge stills of herself
And bright posters announcing events to come.
Her life — she feels it closing about her now
Like a small theater, empty, without lights.

Five Portraits

Portrait with Short Hair

The days, the days!
And the scissors you cut
Your hair with – oh, how dull.
Time to change the needle.

Put on another record –
No, something baroque –
And think of the good times.
Think of lakes and rivers.

It's hot. Let in some air.
Let the smell of leftovers
Be one with the perfume
Of cooling asphalt, leaves.

And the nights? Ah, wonderful –
You alone,
Alone with the slums,
The flowerpots, the stars.

Think of the sea. Unzip,
Just as though someone were
Around to be made love to,
Or anyway to pose for.

The mysteries of sex!
Some day you'll wake up
Back on that Christmas morning
In Mexico, still a virgin.

What lonely aisles you prowled
In search of the forbidden,
Blinking your usher's torch,
Firefly of the balconies!

And when you found it – love! –
It was to pure French horns
Soaring above the plains
Of Saturday's Westerns.

The defiant eyes laughing
Into the sudden beam,
The soft Mexican curses.
The stains, the crushed corsages. . .

Off, off with those bright buttons,
Poor spy. Your heart's as dark
As theirs was and it speaks
With the same broken accent.

Girls read it in your eyes now
And ask for your autograph.
They torture you for secrets.
And you give them poems,

Poems with hair slicked back,
Smelling of bay rum, sweat,
And hot buttered popcorn.
Furtive illuminations. . .

Pull down the shades.
Your black boyfriend is coming.
He's not like you. He wants
To live in the suburbs.

You'd rather paint. Then let
Your hand dream for you,
The same hand, braceleted with scars,
That smooths down cats, sheets, men.

Under it your body
Turns into landscape — look!
Some metamorphosis
Of the moon . . . The ancients

Who watch you from their porches —
You in your earrings, in
Your bare feet, in that long
Boy's undershirt you wear

(Because your breasts are small) —
They're all asleep now,
The insects, the wind . . .
It's late. But then he's married,

And this is still Texas.
The night is a giant cactus.
Potent, aromatic,
The liquors you press from it.

Portrait with One Eye
   for RBV

They robbed you of your ticket
To the revolution, oh,
And then they stomped you good.
But nothing stops you.

You have identified yourself
To the police as quote
Lyric poet. What else? —
With fractured jaw. Orpheus,

Imperishable liar!
Your life's a poem still,
Broken iambs and all,
Jazz, jails — the complete works.

And one blue-silver line
Beyond the Antilles,
Vanishing. . . All fragments.
You who could scream across

The square in Cuernavaca,
At a friend you hadn't seen
For years, the one word, *bitch*,
And turn away — that's style!

Or this, your other voice,
This whisper along the wires
At night, like a dry wind,
Like conscience, always collect.

Self-Portrait as Still Life

The melon on the table,
Plump, unspoiled.
Close by, the knife,
Patient lover.

It smiles. It knows
How attractive it is
To sunlight. It can wait.
The guitar on the wall,

Succumbing to shadow,
To drowsiness, to dream,
Remembering hands,
Beginning to dance now

Somewhere inside,
There, there where the heart's
Most resonant, most empty. . .
And where am I? I don't

Come into the picture.
Poets, O fellow exiles,
Lisping your pure Spanish,
It's your scene now, and welcome.

You take up the guitar.
You cut up the melon.
Myself, I'm not about to
Disturb the composition.

Lethargy

It smiles to see me
Still in my bathrobe.

It sits in my lap
And will not let me rise.

Now it is kissing my eyes.
Arms enfold me, arms

Pale with a thick down.
It seems I am falling asleep

To the sound of a story
Being read me.

This is the story.
Weeks have passed

Since first I lifted my hand
To set it down.

Luxury

You are like a sun of the tropics
Peering through blinds

Drawn for siesta.
Already you teach me

The Spanish for sunflower.
You, alone on the clean sheet.

You, like the spilt moon.
You, like a star

Hidden by sun–goggles.
You shall have a thousand lovers.

You, spread here like butter,
Like doubloons, like flowers.

Sleepily, the muse to me: 'Let us be friends.
Good friends, but only friends. You understand.'
And yawned. And kissed, for the last time, my ear.
Who earlier, weeping at my touch, had whispered:
'I loved you once.' And: 'No, I don't love him.
Not after everything he did.' Later,
Rebuttoning her nightgown with my help:
'Sorry, I just have no desire, it seems.'
Sighing: 'For you, I mean.' Long silence. Then:
'You always were so serious.' At which
I smiled, darkly. And that was how I came
To sleep beside, not with her; without dreams.

I call her up sometimes, long distance now.
And she still knows my voice, but I can hear,
Always beyond the music of her phonograph,
The laughter of the young men with their keys.

I have the number written down somewhere.

Twenty Questions

Is it raining out?
Is it raining in?
Are you a public fountain?
Are you an antique musical instrument?
Are you a famous resort perhaps?
What is your occupation?
Are you by chance a body of water?
Do you often travel alone?
What is your native language then?
Do you recall the word for carnation?

Are you sorry?
Will you be sorry?
Is this your handkerchief?
What is your destination?
Are you Aquarius?
Are you the watermelon flower?
Will you please take off your glasses?
Is this a holiday for you?
Is that a scar, or a birthmark?
Is there some word for calyx in your tongue?

Tell me if you were not happy in those days.
You were not yet twenty-five,
And you had not yet abandoned the guitar.

I swore to you by your nakedness that you were a guitar,
You swore to me by your nakedness that you were a guitar,
The moon swore to us both by your nakedness that you had
    abandoned yourself completely.

Who would not go on living?

The typewriter will be glad to have become the poem,
The guitar to have been your body,
I to have had the luck to envy the sole of your shoe in
    the dead of winter.

A passenger has lost his claim-check
The brunette her barrette,
And I — I think that there are moths eating holes in my pockets,
That my place in line is evaporating,
That the moon is not the moon and the bus is not the bus.

What is the word for goodbye?

White Notes

1

Suddenly there was a dress,
Inhabited, in motion.

It contained a forest,
Small birds, rivers.

It contained the ivory
Of piano keys,
White notes.

Across the back of a chair
Skins of animals
Dried in the moon.

2

It happened.
Your body went out of your body.

It rose
To let the air in,
The night.

From the sheets it rose,
From the bare floor,
Floating.

Over roofs,
Smaller and smaller,
Lost.

Entangled now
In the cold arms
Of distant street-lamps.

3
The city forgets where you live.
It wanders through many streets,
And the streets turn, confused,
Upon one another.

Parks have deserted themselves.
All night, awnings are whipped
And cannot remember.

O forgotten umbrella . . .

Darkness saw you, air
Displaced you, words
Erased you.

4
And afterwards,
After the quenching of the street-lamps,
Long after the ivory could have been brought
    back to life by any touch.

Afterwards, when I might have told you
The address of your future.
Long after the future.

When the umbrella had been closed forever.
Then, when not even the moon
Would have the power to bruise you any more.

Then, in another time.

The Confession

You have no name, intimate crime,
Into which I might plunge my hand.
Your knives have entered many pillows,
But you leave nothing behind.

Dressed in the silence you were sworn to,
You passed without recognition.
No door holds you, no mirror;
I am the lone witness.

You have escaped into smoke,
Into the dark mouths of tunnels.
Once in the streets you were safe,
You were one among many.

The Success

He asked for directions, but the street
Was swaying before him drunkenly.
The buildings leaned together. There was some
Conspiracy of drawn curtains against him.

And all around him he could sense the beauty
Of unseen arms, of eyes that slid off elsewhere.
Someone was living his life there, someone
Was turning back sheets meant to receive his body.

This was the address if not the destination.
The moonlight died along his wrist. His hand
Slipped off through the darkness on its stubborn mission,
Roving the row of mailboxes for the name it dreamed.

He entered. The doorman vanished with a nod.
The elevator ascended smoothly to his desire.
The light in the hall, the door against his cheek. . .
He had arrived. He recognized the laughter.

The Assassination

It begins again, the nocturnal pulse.
It courses through the cables laid for it.
It mounts to the chandeliers and beats there, hotly.
We are too close. Too late, we would move back.
We are involved with the surge.

Now it bursts. Now it has been announced.
Now it is being soaked up by newspapers.
Now it is running through the streets.
The crowd has it. The woman selling carnations
And the man in the straw hat stand with it in their shoes.

Here is the red marquee it sheltered under,
Here is the ballroom, here
The sadly various orchestra led
By a single gesture. My arms open.
It enters. Look, we are dancing.

June 5, 1968

TWO

America has so many roads —
On every road, someone lost.
And should we be sorry for the girls
Who will go into labor nine months from tonight?

Should we be sorry for being born
Americans? Here, lost at the crossroads,
Trying to find our place on the map.
So many towns, so many little stars...

America has surrounded us.
And the poems that fell from our mouths
Like stars in August —
Look for them in the Pacific.

After József

Lorcaesques

A song went looking for light
And met itself coming back.

*

The song with nothing to say
Has gone to sleep on my lips.

1

You live west of the mountains;
I, here.
Night comes to you late;
Dawn, early to me.

As you put on your nightgown,
The one embroidered with mountain-flowers,
I stumble from bed,
Wanting my coffee.

2

Near the summit,
We rest on separate rocks, smoking,
And wonder whether the wildflowers
Are worth going on for.

3

Discs for a cough,
A smooth stone for remembrance.

And the man in the old song,
For a single quince out of season,
Sent back a poem that lasted
Three thousand years.

4

In this life I was styled
'Master-of-Tunes.'
Friend, do me a favor:
Scratch out these lines,
To prove my title.

1

Named ambassador
To the High Court of Prose,
He neglects his manners, his dress,
Speaks in a loud voice, at length,
And is everywhere taken
For one of the natives.

2

P. turns to poetry,
In search, once more,
Of the true primitive.

May he locate the tribe,
Master the dialect.

3

Though, as G. says,
We American poets
No longer love words,
It is hard not to remember
What we felt for
Those that betrayed us,
Those we betrayed.

4

And D., they say, no longer
Hennas her nipples.

5

G. maintains that the Adjective somehow pene-
trates the Noun with all that is most private, thereby
becoming the most personal of the parts of speech,
hence the most beautiful.

I, on the contrary, maintain that the Conjunction,
being impersonal, is the more beautiful, and especially
when suppressed.

6

M., opening my diary, found the pages blank.

7

After the overture,
The opera seemed brief.

Riddle

for SD

White of a blind man's eye
I saw rolling.
When the lid closed over,
Dark was twice dark.

Soon I saw glitter
His other eye.
Dew fell then; dark scattered.
What it saw, men saw.

(The Moon and the Sun)

Things

Stone
Hard, but you can polish it.
Precious, it has eyes. Can wound.
Would dance upon water. Sinks.
Stays put. Crushed, becomes a road.

Pillow
Mine to give, mine to offer
No resistance. Mine
To receive you, mine to keep
The shape of our nights.

Mirror
My former friend, my traitor.
My too easily broken.
My still to be escaped from.

Wall
To support this roof.
To stand up. To take
Such weight in the knees. . .
To keep the secret.
To envy no cloud.

Clock
These quiet hands, their gestures,
These circles drawn upon air.
And the whiteness of the face
That attends the unspoken.
This listening of the deaf.

THREE

There are pines that are tall enough
Already. In the distance,
The whining of saws; and needles,
Silently slipping through the chosen cloth.
The stone, then as now, unfelt,
Perfectly weightless. And certain words,
That will come together to mourn,
Waiting, in their dark clothes, apart.

Variations on a Text by Vallejo

Me moriré en Paris con aguacero . . .

I will die in Miami in the sun,
On a day when the sun is very bright,
A day like the days I remember, a day like other days,
A day that nobody knows or remembers yet,
And the sun will be bright then on the dark glasses of strangers
And in the eyes of a few friends from my childhood
And of the surviving cousins by the graveside,
While the diggers, standing apart, in the still shade of the palms,
Rest on their shovels, and smoke,
Speaking in Spanish softly, out of respect.

I think it will be on a Sunday like today,
Except that the sun will be out, the rain will have stopped,
And the wind that today made all the little shrubs kneel down;
And I think it will be a Sunday because today,
When I took out this paper and began to write,
Never before had anything looked so blank,
My life, these words, the paper, the gray Sunday;
And my dog, quivering under a table because of the storm,
Looked up at me, not understanding,
And my son read on without speaking, and my wife slept.

Donald Justice is dead. One Sunday the sun came out,
It shone on the bay, it shone on the white buildings,
The cars moved down the street slowly as always, so many,
Some with their headlights on in spite of the sun,
And after awhile the diggers with their shovels

Walked back to the graveside through the sunlight,
And one of them put his blade into the earth
To lift a few clods of dirt, the black marl of Miami,
And scattered the dirt, and spat,
Turning away abruptly, out of respect.

Poem

This poem is not addressed to you.
You may come into it briefly,
But no one will find you here, no one.
You will have changed before the poem will.

Even while you sit there, unmovable,
You have begun to vanish. And it does not matter.
The p oem will go on without you.
It has the spurious glamor of certain voids.

It is not sad, really, only empty.
Once perhaps it was sad, no one knows why.
It prefers to remember nothing.
Nostalgias were peeled from it long ago.

Your type of beauty has no place here.
Night is the sky over this poem.
It is too black for stars.
And do not look for any illumination.

You neither can nor should understand what it means.
Listen, it comes without guitar,
Neither in rags nor any purple fashion.
And there is nothing in it to comfort you.

Close your eyes, yawn. It will be over soon.
You will forget the poem, but not before
It has forgotten you. And it does not matter.
It has been most beautiful in its erasures.

O bleached mirrors! Oceans of the drowned!
Nor does it matter what you think.
These are not my words now.
This poem is not addressed to you.

1

Hartford is cold today but no colder for your absence.
The rain is green over Avon and, since your death, the sky
Has been blue many times with a blue you did not imagine.

The judges of Key West sit soberly in black
But only because it is their accustomed garb,
And the sea sings with the same voice still, neither serious nor sorry.

The walls past which you walked in your white suit,
Ponderous, pondering French pictures,
Are no less vivid now. Not one is turned to the wall.

The actuarial tables are not upset.
The mail travels back and forth to Ceylon as before.
The gold leaf peels in season and is renewed.

And there are heroes who falter but do not fall,
Or fall without faltering and without fault,
But you were not one of them. Nevertheless,

The poet practicing his scales
Thinks of you as his thumbs slip clumsily under and under,
Avoiding the darker notes.

2

The *the* has become an *a*. The dictionary
Closed at dusk, along with the zoo in the park.

And the wings of the swans are folded now like the sheets
   of a long letter.
Who borrows your French words and postures now?

  3
The opera of the gods is finished,
And the applause is dying.
The chorus will soon be coming down from the clouds.
Even their silence may be understood
As a final platitude of sorts, a summing up.

The tireless dancers have retired at last
To a small apartment on a treeless street.
But, oh, the pas de deux of Eden begins again
On cotsprings creaking like the sun and moon!
The operation of the universe is temporarily suspended.

What has been good? What has been beautiful?
The tuning up or the being put away?
The instruments have nothing more to say.
Now they must sleep on plush and velvet till
Our breath revives them to new flutterings, new adieux;

And to the picnic all the singers come,
Minus their golden costumes, but no less gods for that.
There all quotations from the text apply,
Including the laughter, including the offstage thunder,
Including even this almost human cry.

Sonatina in Green

for my students

One spits on the sublime.
One lies in bed alone, reading
Yesterday's newspaper. One
Has composed a beginning, say,
A phrase or two. No more!
There has been traffic enough
In the boudoir of the muse.

And still they come, demanding entrance,
Noisy, and with ecstatic cries
Catching the perfume, forcing their way —
For them, what music? Only,
Distantly, through some door ajar,
Echoes, broken strains; and the garland
Crushed at the threshold.

                              And we,
We few with the old instruments,
Obstinate, sounding the one string —
For us, what? Only, at times,
The sunlight of late afternoon
That plays in the corner of a room,
Playing upon worn keys. At times,
Smells of decaying greenery, faint bouquets —
More than enough. And our cries
Diminish behind us:

                              Cover
The bird cages! No more

Bargain days in the flower stalls!
There has been traffic enough
In the boudoir of the muse,
More than enough traffic.
                    Or say
That one composed, in the end,
Another beginning, in spite of all this
Sublime. Enough!

Closed are the grand boulevards,
And closed those mouths that made the lesser songs,
And the curtains drawn in the boudoir.

Sonatina in Yellow

Du schnell vergehendes Daguerreotyp
in meinen langsamer vergehenden Händen. — Rilke

The pages of the album,
As they are turned, turn yellow; a word,
Once spoken, obsolete,
No longer what was meant. Say it.
The meanings come, or come back later,
Unobtrusive, taking their places.

Think of the past. Think of forgetting the past.
It was an exercise requiring further practice;
A difficult exercise, played through by someone else.
Overheard from another room, now,
It seems full of mistakes.
                                    So the voice of your father,
Rising as from the next room still
With all the remote but true affection of the dead,
Repeats itself, insists,
Insisting you must listen, rises
In the familiar pattern of reproof
For some childish error, a nap disturbed,
Or vase, broken or overturned;
Rises and subsides. And you do listen.
Listen and forget. Practice forgetting.

Forgotten sunlight still
Blinds the eyes of faces in the album.
The faces fade, and there is only

A sort of meaning that comes back,
Or for the first time comes, but comes too late
To take the places of the faces.

                    Remember
The dead air of summer. Remember
The trees drawn up to their full height like fathers,
The underworld of shade you entered at their feet.
Enter the next room. Enter it quietly now,
Not to disturb your father sleeping there. *He stirs.*
Notice his clothes, how scrupulously clean,
Unwrinkled from the nap; his face, freckled with work,
Smoothed by a passing dream. The vase
Is not yet broken, the still young roses
Drink there from perpetual waters. *He rises, speaks...*

Repeat it now, no one was listening.
Repeat it, the air, the variations.
So your hand moves, moving across the keys,
And slowly the keys grow darker to the touch.

Three Odes

Cool Dark Ode

You could have sneaked up,
Broken into those underheated rooms
By the windows overlooking the tavern,
Or the back way, up the broad but unlighted stairs,
At a moment when no one was present,
When the long planed table that served as a desk
Was recalling the quiet of the woods,
When the books, older, were thinking farther back,
To the same essential stillness,
And both table and books, if they thought of the future ever,
Probably shuddered, as though from a stray draft,
Seeing themselves as eventual flame,
Some final smoke.

Now, when there is no longer any occasion,
I think of inviting you in
To wait for us
On the short, cramped sofa,
Beside the single candle-stub
Which must have frightened you off then,
Or in the cubicle of the bedroom,
Where even then we imagined ourselves extinguished
By your total embrace,
Attentive meanwhile to the animal noises of your breathing,
The whimpers,
The sudden intoxicated outcries,
That were not our own.

Night, night, O blackness of winter,
I tell you this, you
That used to come up as far as the frosted panes, the door,
As far as the edges of our skin,
Without any thought, I know now,
Of entering those borrowed rooms,
Or even our mouths, our eyes,
Which all too often were carelessly left open for you.

It was still possible then
To imagine that no more than one or two hands
Would ever move down the face of the hour,
And that the shadow which followed
Might remain patient
And, if anything, somewhat reluctant to continue;
That no more than one or two hands
Had ever descended so far
As the shoulders of the afternoon,
And that, necessarily, they would have been bare then
Of even that shadow which, sometimes, the air itself seems
    to be charged with
And to suffer from;
That no more than one or two hands surely
Would have crossed the forbidden zone
At the end of summer,
And that the sky there would be turning always from white
    to pink, slowly,
And that it could no longer matter then
What shadows rose from your hollows and sank back.

And it is still possible to imagine
That there are one or two hands
Which do not know, or which do not yet know,
Anything of either that face or the shadow
Which does, after all, follow,
Or of flushed shoulders or turning sky,
Or of those particular hollows, alive
With less and less curious and impulsive shadows now;
And that there may somewhere be hands

Which will never be smeared with the very special pollen
And general muskiness of a dying summer;
And that there are probably other hands which have stopped,
Or will stop, or even now are shaken with premonitions
Of a time when they will have begun to stop,
And among these some which remember little or nothing
Of you and your coloring,
And some also which do not and cannot forget
Your blood upon them and your dew.

Not with the vague smoke
In the curtains,
Not with the pigeons or doves
Under the eaves,
Nevertheless you are there, hidden,
And again you wake me,
Scentless, noiseless,
Someone or something,
Something or someone faithless,
And that will not return.

Undiscovered star,
That fade and are fading,
But never entirely fading,
Fixed,
And that will not return.

Someone, someone or something,
Colorless, formless,
And that will not return.

It's snowing this afternoon and there are no flowers,
There is only this sound of falling, quiet and remote,
Like the memory of scales descending the white keys
Of a childhood piano — outside the window, palms!
And the heavy head of the cereus, inclining,
Soon to let down its white or yellow-white.

Now, only these poor snow-flowers in a heap,
Like the memory of a white dress cast down...
So much has fallen.
                    And I, who have listened for a step
All afternoon, hear it now, but already falling away,
Already in memory. And the terrible scales descending
On the silent piano; the snow; and the absent flowers abounding.

Everyone, everyone went away today.
They left without a word, and I think
I did not hear a single goodbye today.

And all that I saw was someone's hand, I think,
Thrown up out there like the hand of someone drowning,
But far away, too far to be sure what it was or meant.

No, but I saw how everything had changed
Later, just as the light had; and at night
I saw that from dream to dream everything changed.

And those who might have come to me in the night,
The ones who did come back but without a word,
All those I remembered passed through my hands like clouds —

Clouds out of the south, familiar clouds —
But I could not hold onto them, they were drifting away,
Everything going away in the night again and again.

Notes

'The Confession', 'The Success', 'The Assassination', 'Clock' (from 'Things'), and the sonatinas come, in part, from chance methods.

'On the Night of the Departure by Bus' and 'Cool Dark Ode' are loosely modeled, in structure, on poems by Rafael Alberti. See 'En el día de su muerte a mano armada' and the fourth part of 'Colegio (S.J.).' The first two lines, the last line, and perhaps others in 'White Notes' were also suggested by passages in Alberti's *Sobre los ángeles*.

Some images in 'B' are adapted from a series of poems by Guillevic (*Choses*). Most of the events and images in 'A Dancer's Life' were remembered, perhaps wrongly, from Bergman movies, scripts, and criticism.

'1971' is a departure from a translation by John Batki of Attila József. The remote sources for 'After the Chinese' appear in *The Penguin Book of Chinese Verse* (Yang Wan-Li, Wang Chia, Ch'in Chia, and Chëng-Yen). 'Riddle' is based on a well-known Old English riddle.

The Stevens poem follows a performance of Edward Miller's opera, *The Young God*, in Hartford, Spring, 1969.

Donald Justice

Donald Justice was born in Miami, Florida, in 1925 and grew up there. After attending the University of Miami, he studied at the University of North Carolina, Stanford, and Iowa. He has taught at a number of universities, including Syracuse and the University of California (Irvine), as well as Iowa, where he now teaches. His first book, *The Summer Anniversaries*, was the Lamont poetry selection for 1959. He has also published *Night Light* (1967) and was the editor of *The Collected Poems of Weldon Kees* (1960) and co-editor, with Alexander Aspel, of *Contemporary French Poetry* (1965). He has received grants in poetry from The Rockefeller Foundation and from the National Council on the Arts, and in theater from The Ford Foundation. He is married and has one son, Nathaniel.